D1120113

I SEE SEA FOOD

For my parents, Claudia and Joe—thank you for filling my childhood with books. For my favorite reading buddies, Tessa and Tanner. And for Shawn, because you knew I could.

The author would like to thank the following people for generously sharing their knowledge and expertise: Giacomo Bernardi, Professor, UC Santa Cruz; Prosanta Chakrabarty, PhD, Curator of Fishes/Associate Professor, Louisiana State University; Christopher Mah, PhD, Research Associate, Department of Invertebrate Zoology, Smithsonian National Museum of Natural History; Mark McGrouther, Senior Fellow, Ichthyology, Australian Museum Research Institute; Wyatt Patry, Senior Aquarist, Monterey Bay Aquarium; and Ángel A. Valdés, PhD, Biology Professor, California State Polytechnic University.

Millbrook Press™
An imprint of Lerner Publishing Group, Inc.
241 First Avenue North
Minneapolis, MN 55401 USA

For reading levels and more information, look up this title at www.lernerbooks.com.

Main body text set in Adderville ITC Std.
Typeface provided by International Typeface Corp.

Library of Congress Cataloging-in-Publication Data

Names: Grodzicki, Jenna, 1979– author.
Title: I see sea food : sea creatures that look like food / Jenna Grodzicki.
Description: Minneapolis : Millbrook Press, [2020] | Audience: Age 4–9. | Audience: K to Grade 3. | Includes bibliographical references.
Identifiers: LCCN 2018049344 (print) | LCCN 2018051533 (ebook) | ISBN 9781541562639 (eb pdf) | ISBN 9781541554634 (lib. bdg. : alk. paper) | ISBN 9781541562639 (epdf)
Subjects: LCSH: Marine animals—Adaptation—Juvenile literature.
Classification: LCC QL122.2 (ebook) | LCC QL122.2 .G77 2020 (print) | DDC 591.77—dc23

LC record available at https://lccn.loc.gov/2018049344

Manufactured in the United States of America
1-45781-42663-3/25/2019

I SEE SEA FOOD

SEA CREATURES THAT LOOK LIKE FOOD

JENNA GRODZICKI

M Millbrook Press/Minneapolis

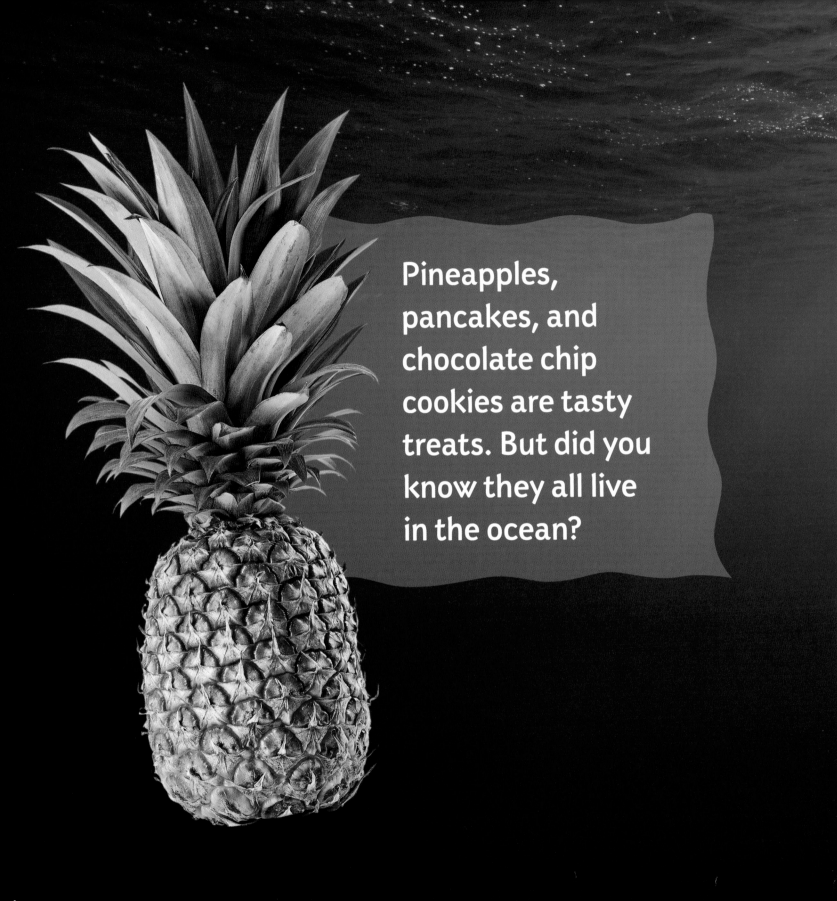

Pineapples, pancakes, and chocolate chip cookies are tasty treats. But did you know they all live in the ocean?

THAT CAN'T BE RIGHT!

OR IS IT?

These sea creatures aren't your normal seafood. These weird and wonderful animals look a lot like the foods we know and love.

But their appetizing appearance isn't just for fun. Each animal has reasons for having features that happen to look like their tasty twins.

An AUSTRALIAN PINEAPPLEFISH swims slowly through the coral reef.

8

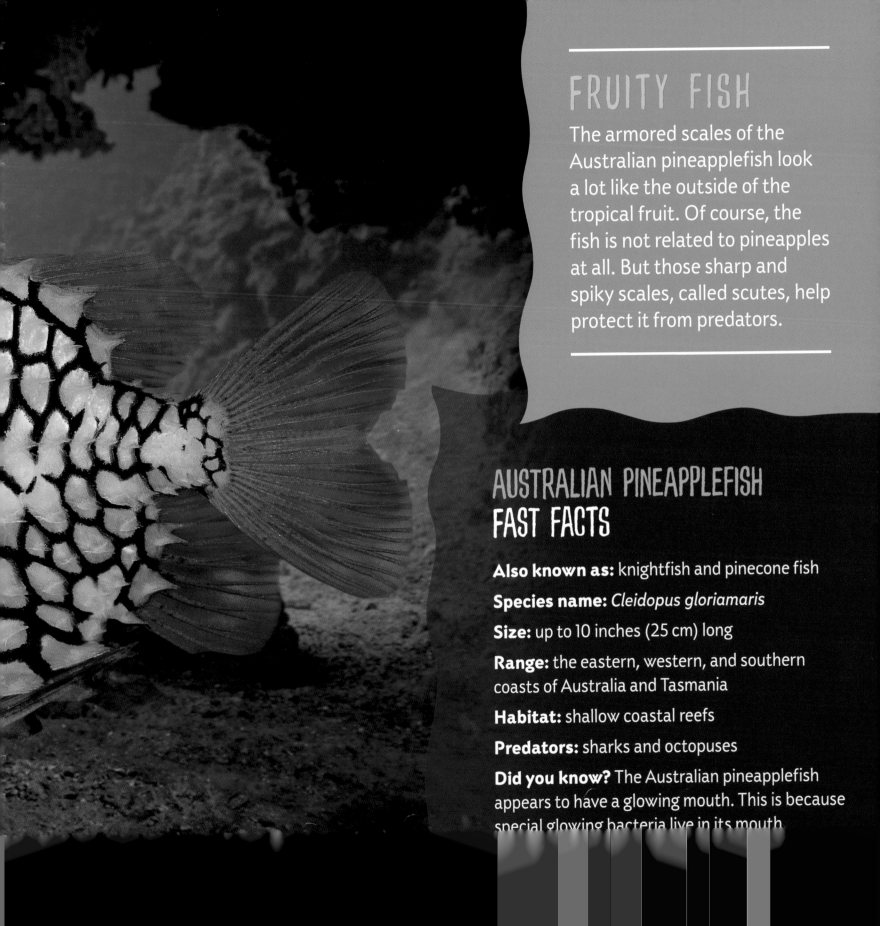

FRUITY FISH

The armored scales of the Australian pineapplefish look a lot like the outside of the tropical fruit. Of course, the fish is not related to pineapples at all. But those sharp and spiky scales, called scutes, help protect it from predators.

AUSTRALIAN PINEAPPLEFISH FAST FACTS

Also known as: knightfish and pinecone fish

Species name: *Cleidopus gloriamaris*

Size: up to 10 inches (25 cm) long

Range: the eastern, western, and southern coasts of Australia and Tasmania

Habitat: shallow coastal reefs

Predators: sharks and octopuses

Did you know? The Australian pineapplefish appears to have a glowing mouth. This is because special glowing bacteria live in its mouth.

An EGG YOLK JELLYFISH drifts along with the tide.

SUNNY-SIDE UP

The delicate bell of the egg yolk jellyfish looks like a freshly cracked egg in the water. The egg yolk jelly dines on other jellyfish, and it takes on the color of its prey. If the bell is white and yellow, the egg yolk jellyfish has been munching on moon jellies. But if it's more orange in appearance, you can bet it's been feeding on sea nettles.

EGG YOLK JELLYFISH FAST FACTS

Also known as: fried egg jellyfish

Species name: *Phacellophora camtschatica*

Size: bell diameter of 0.7 to 2 feet (0.2 to 0.6 m) and tentacle lengths of 10 to 20 feet (3 to 6 m) long

Range: the eastern Pacific Ocean

Habitat: cold waters

Predators: sea turtles, more than fifty species of fish, other jellyfish, and some marine birds

Did you know? An egg yolk jellyfish can have hundreds of tentacles.

A constellation of CHOCOLATE CHIP SEA STARS spreads out across the ocean floor.

MILK AND COOKIES

Dark brown, pointy horns that look like chocolate chips cover the chocolate chip sea star. But those horns aren't there to remind us of freshly baked cookies. They act like armor to help prevent hungry fish from taking a bite.

CHOCOLATE CHIP SEA STAR
FAST FACTS

Also known as: the horned starfish

Species name: *Protoreaster nodosus*

Size: 8 to 16 inches (20 to 40 cm) long

Range: the Pacific Ocean, the Indian Ocean, and the Red Sea

Habitat: sandy and muddy lagoons and seagrass beds in warm, shallow waters

Predators: triggerfish, puffer fish, boxfish, and parrotfish

Did you know? No two chocolate chip sea stars are exactly alike.

A BANANA WRASSE swims in and out of the nooks and crannies of the reef.

BANANA SPLIT

A wrasse is a type of fish with thick lips and strong teeth. You might mistake this creature for a banana that's ripe for the peeling. But it's not a fruit at all. All female banana wrasses have banana-colored scales. The males are rainbow colored. The difference in coloring makes it easier for banana wrasses to find mates.

BANANA WRASSE FAST FACTS

Also known as: yellow-brown wrasse, sunset wrasse, and yellow wrasse

Species name: *Thalassoma lutescens*

Size: 9 to 12 inches (23 to 30 cm) long

Range: the Indian Ocean, Hawaiian Islands, south and southeastern Australia, and the western Pacific Ocean

Habitat: warm, shallow coastal waters, rocky reefs, and coral reefs

Predators: larger fish

Did you know? There are more than five hundred species of wrasses including the banana wrasse.

A LETTUCE SEA SLUG creeps along the coral.

ALL-YOU-CAN-EAT SALAD BAR

The lettuce sea slug's ruffled "leaves," or parapodia, look a lot like the lettuce it's named after. This sea slug has a unique way of eating. First, it dines on algae. Then the lettuce sea slug uses a tiny part of the algae called the chloroplast to perform photosynthesis. The chloroplasts are stored inside the parapodia. They capture sunlight and use the light to make sugar. The sugar then helps feed the sea slug. The chloroplasts also give the lettuce sea slug its green hue.

LETTUCE SEA SLUG
FAST FACTS

Also known as: crawling leaf slug

Species name: *Elysia crispata*

Size: up to 2 inches (5 cm) long

Range: the Caribbean Sea from the Florida Keys to Bermuda

Habitat: shallow waters in tropical reefs

Predators: no known predators

Did you know? The ruffled shape of the parapodia helps the sea slug get as much sunlight as possible.

A LOUISIANA PANCAKE BATFISH swims near the bottom of the ocean.

PASS THE SYRUP

The Louisiana pancake batfish is small, round, and flat, just like a pancake. Its skin is bumpy and looks like a pancake that was left sitting out for too long. The pancake-like shape and coloring of this fish provide camouflage. The Louisiana pancake batfish lies on the ocean floor to hide from predators.

LOUISIANA PANCAKE BATFISH FAST FACTS

Also known as: tortilla fish

Species name: *Halieutichthys intermedius*

Size: up to 4 inches (10 cm) long

Range: the Gulf of Mexico and parts of the Southern Atlantic by Georgia, Florida, and the Carolinas

Habitat: seabeds in deep waters

Predators: marlins, tuna, and other fish

Did you know? The Louisiana pancake batfish uses its fins to walk along the ocean floor.

A SEA APPLE perches on the coral reef.

RED DELICIOUS

The colorful sea apple is not a fruit at all. It's a type of animal known as a sea cucumber. Sea cucumbers are oval-shaped ocean animals with tough, spiny, bumpy skin. The sea apple is shaped like an oval most of the time. But when it senses danger, it sucks in a large amount of water. This causes the sea apple's body to inflate into a round shape, and it quickly floats away.

SEA APPLE FAST FACTS

Also known as: violet sea cucumber

Species name: *Pseudocolochirus violaceus*

Size: 4 to 8 inches (10 to 20 cm) long

Range: the Indian Ocean and western part of the Pacific Ocean

Habitat: coral reefs in tropical waters

Predators: some kinds of fish

Did you know? Sea apples breathe through their butts.

The **CAULIFLOWER JELLYFISH** swims through the open ocean with its long filaments trailing behind.

JUST ADD BUTTER

The cauliflower jellyfish may remind you to eat your vegetables. It has large, curly arms that look like the cauliflower on your dinner plate. Without these arms, the cauliflower jellyfish would go hungry. The arms collect tiny animals from the water. Then the cauliflower jellyfish sends the food up into its four stomachs.

CAULIFLOWER JELLYFISH FAST FACTS

Also known as: crown jellyfish

Species name: *Cephea cephea*

Size: bell 20 to 24 inches (50 to 60 cm) in diameter

Range: the Tropical Pacific, the Indian Ocean, and the Red Sea

Habitat: open waters

Predators: sea turtles and other jellyfish

Did you know? A cauliflower jellyfish has no heart, brain, or blood.

A **PIZZA CRUST SEA SLUG** inches along the rocky reef.

EXTRA CHEESE, PLEASE

If you saw this creature, you might think someone dropped a piece of pizza on the ocean floor. But it's really a sea slug. The pizza crust sea slug is covered in small round bumps called tubercles. These tubercles look a lot like bits of cheese and pepperoni. Scientists believe its coloring and shape could help the pizza crust sea slug blend into its environment.

PIZZA CRUST SEA SLUG
FAST FACTS

Also known as: Atlantic sidegill slug, or warty sidegill slug

Species name: *Pleurobranchus areolatus*

Size: 1.2 to 2 inches (3 to 5 cm) long

Range: the tropical western Atlantic

Habitat: rocky reefs

Predators: no known predators

Did you know? A pizza crust sea slug has a shell on the inside of its body.

Thousands of creatures of all shapes and sizes live in the world's oceans. Scientists believe there are many more out there that have yet to be discovered.

But when it comes to ocean animals, sharks, dolphins, whales, and sea turtles get most of the attention. The weird and wonderful sea creatures deserve some love too!

Maybe this list of sea food look-alikes
will continue to grow.

THE NEXT DISCOVERY COULD BE YOURS!

GLOSSARY

algae (AL-jee): plantlike living things that use sunlight to make their food. Seaweed is a type of algae.

bell: the umbrellalike body of a jellyfish

camouflage (KAM-uh-flahzh): a way of hiding something by covering or coloring it so it looks like its surroundings

chloroplast (KLOR-uh-plast): a structure found in plants and algae that helps turn sunlight into usable energy

filaments (FIL-uh-muhnts): thin, threadlike attachments

mate: a member of an animal pair that breeds to produce babies

parapodia (par-uh-POH-dee-uh): ruffled flaps of tissue on the lettuce sea slug that look like leaves

photosynthesis (foh-tuh-SIN-thuh-sihs): the process by which plants (and the lettuce sea slug) take energy from the sun and change it into food

predator (PRED-uh-tur): an animal that gets its food by eating other animals

prey: an animal that is hunted and killed by another animal for food

range: the geographical area where a species lives

scutes (skoots): bony plates or scales

sea cucumber: ocean animals shaped like cylinders with tough, spiny, bumpy skin

species: a group of similar living things that are able to mate and produce offspring with one another

tentacles (TEN-tuh-khuls): the long, flexible armlike parts of an animal that stick out around its head or mouth and are used for grabbing things and moving

tubercles (TOO-bur-khuls): small lumps, or bumps

SEA FOOD OR ME FOOD?

Can you tell the difference between the food you'd expect to see on your plate and the creatures living in the ocean? Check the next page to see if you guessed right.

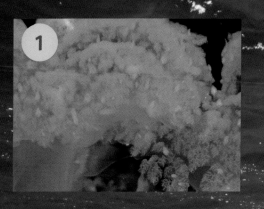

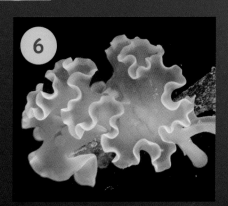

FURTHER READING

Beck, W. H. *Glow: Animals with Their Own Night-Lights.* New York: Houghton Mifflin Harcourt, 2016.

Chin, Jason. *Coral Reefs.* New York: Roaring Brook, 2011.

Hughes, Catherine D. *First Big Book of the Ocean.* Washington, DC: National Geographic Kids, 2013.

Keating, Jess. *What Makes a Monster? Discovering the World's Scariest Creatures.* New York: Alfred A. Knopf, 2017.

Keating, Jess. *Cute as an Axolotl: Discovering the World's Most Adorable Animals.* New York: Alfred A. Knopf, 2018.

Marsh, Laura. *Weird Sea Creatures.* Washington, DC: National Geographic, 2012.

PHOTO ACKNOWLEDGMENTS

Image credits: Nadeika/iStock/Getty Images, pp. 2–3, 4–5, 31 (background); baibaz/iStock/Getty Images, p. 4 (pineapple); Africa Studio/Shutterstock.com, pp. 5 (pancakes), 31 (5); p_saranya/iStock/Getty Images, p. 5 (cookies); Paulo Oliveira/Alamy Stock Photo, pp. 6, 8–9; Prosanta Chakrabarty, Ph.D./LSU Museum of Natural Science, p. 7 (top); Nature Picture Library/Alamy Stock Photo, p. 7 (bottom); WaterFrame/Alamy Stock Photo, pp. 10, 22–23; Norbert Probst/imageBROKER/Alamy Stock Photo, pp. 12–13; marrio31/iStock/Getty Images, pp. 14–15; Reinhard Dirscherl/Alamy Stock Photo, pp. 16–17; Natalie Ruffing/iStock/Getty Images, pp. 18–19 (background); SEFSC Pascagoula Laboratory; Collection of Brandi Noble, NOAA/NMFS/SEFSC/Flickr (public domain), pp. 18–19 (batfish); Ethan Daniels/Shutterstock.com, pp. 20–21; Andrew J. Martinez/Science Source, pp. 24–25; feathercollector/Shutterstock.com, p. 26 (yellow wrasse); Levent Konuk/Shutterstock.com, pp. 26–27 (jellyfish); age fotostock/Alamy Stock Photo, p. 26 (sea apple); johnandersonphoto/iStock/Getty Images, p. 27 (lettuce sea slug); Spondylolithesis/iStock/Getty Images, p. 27 (egg-yolk jellyfish); Borisoff/Shutterstock.com, pp. 28–29; Mark Conlin/Oxford Scientific/Getty Images, p. 31 (1); Lea Lee/Moment Open/Getty Images, p. 31 (2); wwing/iStock/Getty Images, p. 31 (3); triocea/iStock/Getty Images, p. 31 (4); Christian Ziegler/Minden Pictures, p. 31 (6); solidcolours/iStock/Getty Images. p. 37 (7).

Cover: John Rusk/Flickr (CC BY 2.0).

Answers to Sea Food or Me Food: 1. sea food; 2. sea food; 3. me food, 4. me food; 5. me food; 6. sea food; 7. me food